FIRSTMATTERPRESS

Portland, Ore.

YOU ARE AN AMBIGUOUS PRONOUN

k.m. lighthouse

FIRSTMATTERPRESS

Portland, Ore.

Published in the United States
by First Matter Press
Portland, Oregon

"Composition" was first published in *From Sac*.

Paperback ISBN 978-0-9972987-3-4

Cover Illustration Copyright © 2010
by Holger Lippmann www.lumicon.de
The Engraving Series #1, generative digital art

Book design & typography
by Ash Good www.ashgood.design

Dedicated to you herein.
You know who you are.

CONTENTS

YOU
ARE AN
AMBIGUOUS
PRONOUN

To Eitan,
Thank you for the
inspiration, and
support!

PROLOGUE

You will fascinate the poet, and the poet will want to experience
all of you. In doing so, the poet becomes a reflection of you,
the relationship now two mirrors exchanging glances on and
on indefinitely until you are in love with yourself.

You will lose yourself in your body with the poet. The poet
will ask you to lie uncomfortably still until you believe the two
of you are one being—at least, until the poet pulls away and—
still naked—pulls out a notebook.

IDENTITY CRISIS IN A UNISEX BATHROOM

While I'm in here,
I can't help but remember you, the one afraid of looking
too much like a man.
Your lips didn't quite curve right
around mine because you interrupted—
I've always wondered what it would be like to kiss...
   you.
See? Not that different—
but that was before I learned
no one says I look tired if I wear mascara
and lipstick—long-lasting so I can kiss and sleep
and go to the dentist and give head.

But then there's you, the boisterous monkey-woman who spoke
no words for three hours
while we danced—you in '90s music video
cargo pants unbuttoned once—who later held my hand
while we had sex with men and they didn't know
which one was mine.
And then there's you, who didn't mind
that the others were beautiful because none
of you look alike.

Perhaps I would still know you
if I were a man
            or
if I could change my sex as often
as I change underwear and shower—
three times a day because of this goddamn yeast
infection. I'd spread my legs
in a space of masculinity and strut
like I own this place,
but I can't erase this lipstick,
so I'll tangle myself with a man—a person-drug
to throw my body against to prove I am not delicate.
I'll gain his powers like Salmacis did
before I swim in all the pools in Turkey to forget
I'm a woman.
Except, Turkey is $2,000 away,
so I'll stay in the bathroom again;
it doesn't have a gender so I can go in one
and walk out another.

When I want to crawl back into my mother's womb
and come out
another person, that's when I call her—
I am the miscarried boy she birthed before me,
and in the blurry disposable camera
photos that sat too long,
I look wrong against my dad's Harley—
ripped American flag painted up the side—
I would have posed better as that boy. Take me
as Aphrodite's daughter, son
of Hermes, or better yet, strip me down
to nothing
and no one so I can go
and come as I please.

COMPOSITION

Call it mutually assured destruction—
                              a terrible break
of what makes a person
to become what makes a poet.

I drop pieces—   poems—
                    of my body
where I'd like to return,
words,   phrases,   feelings like bookmarks
tied to locations,   and more notably, you.

Perhaps we only appropriate intimacy;
after all, doesn't it live
            in psoriasis-covered knees
and cracking elbows?
No,   medication won't help.

We knew that— we knew that
when I first recognized your skin—
                              armadillo plates
more hardened and darkened than mine,
            when I learned to shove
            my hand between your armor
            and confiscate your heart,   which
                    when pulled,   tugged on my own.

Our fault lines—   lives
scattered like shale beneath
an oil drill that blends
and mars the integrity
of the ground—   compose
our personal landslide into obscurity.

And in your own attempts at avalanche—
          so perfectly engineered
     in piles
     of snow and dynamite—
I,   too,   risk full submersion,
and,   in submersion,   anonymity.

KINTSUGI

I wake up before you,
the shower your alarm clock,
except
this time,
you don't turn
the water cold while you kiss me.

You take the soap from me, flecked
with wood flakes so I smell like you.
Later, bar in hand,
I trail dollar-store bubbles down
your hardened calves
until
we reappear as men
in ancient public baths—early
morning or late night,
the moon's craters
larger than we remember—
and I forget
myself in your service.

We return
to your bed,
clean,
dry, and I trace your left arm past
capillaries, veins to the cracks
and your gold-filled
fractures.

I pour
aurumic light
through joined fingers
before you say,
Pottery was once broken
as an excuse
to fill gaps,
and I think, soon, you'll be only
one color,
the water between your cells
replaced with liquid gold.

I WOULD WAIT FOR YOU AS A MAN IN ROME, BUT AS A WOMAN, I'M A RUNNER

We walk through the gardens
at well-past closing

There   we find seams   cracks in sidewalks
             hungry to cut us from the pattern

We never blend well enough
                   for reality's greedy solipsist

so we steal rose petals and tie sachets
to the caverns of our minds

We spend our afternoons in bed
while overcast light   enough to melt
                         the dusted snow   beckons
an early darkness   I trace
constellations down your right arm
           signing my name in lights and stars
                      arrows and matchsticks

Here   we are both secrets   doors and keys
for a 12-foot-square piece of universe

When you resonate with my syllables
        I am met with the closed eyes of hiding smiles
            but they sneak out in your sleep

With your head near my open hands
        you pour forth from the fortress of

subconsciousness

There is power in vulnerability
        where ours is an entanglement
        beyond convention
            an involvement without the breath
                  of punctuation

HOLDING PATTERN

Anxiety dreams in lines of verse—
but in three or four hours, your alarm
will sound.

Once, when I wandered
the apartment, the door *was* unlocked,
but my insomnia is make-believe,
temporary, surely period-induced,
medication-inspired. Conditions
such as these must start somewhere.

I wear dark eye-circles
like trophies; I'm a real
poet now at odds with my body.
I drink my fourth glass of water—liquid
sloshing in my distended belly—
and return to stretch into big spoon.
I turn away in restlessness,
but you sleep so deeply.

ROUND-TRIP TICKET

The TSA
agent asks if everything is okay

        but I don't want
                another man's pat down

I'm fine
Everything's fine   and he ushers
                me through the precheck line.

You might find the postcards
I didn't bother to mail   scattered
                in the still-packed boxes of the bedroom

where we forgot how to sleep alone

                I didn't want such bare-faced admissions
                in the hands of pilot mailmen
                      roommate parents

But   then again   I never liked envelopes
          or
          egg cartons
            or
            airplanes

I try to call when I know
     there will be no answer   and all my thoughts
         sound of dial tones.

OBSCURE OBJECT

Perhaps I only know you
as a series of curated objects:

yellowed pages, blank skin
bound with string and metal,

coins collected from cultures
assumed and appropriated—reduced
to gift shop pocket charms.

Here, a shirt—uncertainly
yours—that smells of wool and work
and weather,

and over here
an etched reproduction of your hand,
transcribed and translated in panes
of glass.

Except, perhaps museums, too,
contain truth;

the orb swaddled here
in royal purple velvet

maintains within the nebulous
black fog:
the color of
your eyes in dim light.

In my unwrapping,
I know you feel these whispers—
tremors down a makeshift telephone
of aluminum cans and dental floss.

But, before long,
I replace the orb to the velvet
like a child returns an overdue book.

Both patron and curator,
I fall back among the exhibits—

the clinically white walls
awash with harsh light—

and become another unstudied spectator
you don't remember
you forgot.

WHEN I RETURN FOR PUMPKIN CURRY

The City will force out
these food carts next month in favor
of apartment buildings, but   I listen
in a throng of people long before
others move here.   I listen to impatient minds
and less patient bodies. I listen
to uncomfortable silence wane after a stranger
sits at a table and time labels him
a fixture.   I listen to the violin's homogeneous notes
in the breeze between voices.   I listen
to sounds of unborn babies and the ghost
of you who once sat here
while I sat opposite.   I listen to memories
we didn't know to savor
and children with belled anklets
instead of leashes.   I listen to how easy it is
to find somewhere to sit when you're alone.

ON WEARING THE DIRTY SWEATSHIRT AGAIN

Digging in the laundry basket,
I find the $5 sweatshirt like one my mom wore
in the '90s—perfect because it's black
and covered in cat hair and reminds me
of the day we went crabbing in Newport.

I took that picture from the pier
before darkness found us.
I brought a notebook and pens
but didn't use them. Instead, I took turns
pulling up the pot without a license, feeding
animals to other animals.
No amount of soap and water
would erase crab-bait stench from our fingers.

Low tide—best for crabbing.
Slack tide—best for crabbing.
High tide—best for crabbing.
We didn't know but drank Rogue beer
we didn't like and watched while Zeus gulped
gallons of seawater only to spew
out from both mouth and tail end,
and it was everything
we could do to stop him from doing it again.

That morning in the hotel room we split,
you showed me your breasts—
your brown nipples—and I
pulled down my shirt to show off
my tattoo. I wish I knew then
that you would leave me.

We brought back five crabs that night, left
in a cooler to die immersed in the soundtrack
of someone else's arguments.
We couldn't eat them; they'd been dead too long.

I hear you have a baby now, and I'm
a vegetarian. The sweatshirt still fits,
though I fear it may never get washed.

AN HOUR FROM CANADA

Ten days before I tie my tubes,
I read poems about you aloud and omit nothing;
your meteorite eyes are wet as you say
     I forgot how much I love you,
but I assume you're talking to the baby.

     I thought you always liked women more
you say at the stove—baby over shoulder
like you've always been a mom,
though birth did not change you.

Corn on the cob turns
to mush in boiling water while we wait
for your brother. You're celibate,
you mention twice, and love
being single.
You live on nine acres of solar panels
and straw gardens where we banter
with the baby while our eyes are open.
     Tell me what you've read—I want
     a mind like yours,
so I'll send a book from every genre.

Your stepdad offers your brother as a human
heater twice, once after I say I'm married.
There's a large bottle of cheap table wine,
but I drink your glass
while you pump milk and it squirts
like a sprinkler.

> *I only use wine when I cook—*
> *white wine—only when I cook.*

In the morning, your bare feet and mine
look similar—tiny purple remnants
of nail polish months old—and I am
an armchair for the baby.
We listen to podcasts about bees
on the way to the farmer's market
where we pretend to be lovers
and say *we don't know yet* when vendors ask
if the baby is a boy.

I see spiral shell earrings but don't have cash,
so I use credit for blackberry beet wine and chive plants
whose flowers taste of onions.

You look like you've lost weight
you say in the car, and I have,
but when the breeze is enough for a sweatshirt,
I put on one that reminds me of you,
and in the mirror, I almost look
pregnant.

THE SUN'S OUT ON THE OREGON COAST

and it feels good to wander
the paved path with you to Haystack Rock
that reminds me

of the camping trip
under the sky when there were more
dangling silkworms than stars.
I couldn't have returned
to the ocean alone; you're here
and play the guitar so only the wind
carries the force of it.
On the rocks, barnacles

cut my hands and feet, but the weight
of me leaves no imprint; even the sand
is careful not to let me sink;
perhaps I only exist in your Aviator mirrors.
The beach-cliff fences don't keep us out,
as ethereal as we have become—our bodies

light with the sound of acoustic strings
and phrases no one has said before.
Peering past cliffs,
the sea has long calmed

and leaves debris of me—filtered through the grains
of sand—in the form of broken-bottle sea glass
for someone's windchimes.

Last time I was here,
the storm conjured waves to be afraid of—
the sun takes the violence out of them,
and I don't recognize their shapes.
The wind whistles past your ear and tells me

to visit the womb tree—the one
that covers my hand in sap—
suspended over the path with stubborn roots.
I don't speak,
but you tell me you enjoy
hearing my voice inside you.

SOUTHEAST 28TH AND DIVISION

It is Good Friday
when we read Ash Good's early work
under the stringed star lights of a bohemian
food-cart pod.
The firepit spits coals

when we remember to watch,
but your forehead's cold when I kiss it.
May I kiss your shoulder?
   I nod.
Over or under your coat?
   Under.

You bend to my sweater dress sleeve,
my wool coat shrugged slightly.
I turn
my head toward you and do not move—
afraid to break

the porcelain we have become.
The lack of movement punctuates the poetry
we'd spoken
into the night, more sensual
than the oiled girl I wrestled naked,
or when I danced

with only my hat on.
Here, I do not even bare
my skin, but a man throws
uneaten food in a nearby garbage can
before saying, *that was the most romantic—*
perhaps we needed a witness;
maybe someone else needed

to believe us.
On the way back to the car,
I am grateful for the silence I ask for
with silence.
If you know me at all...
  I know you, et al. (2017).

I finger my wedding ring while you drive
the wrong direction—the seat belt's ding
reminding me I exist.

TRANSLATION

In the jellyfish glow of dawn
    I stand   and my skin sings
           each of my cells with a pair of ears
           to ring independently in a symphony
           of blinding sound.

As my hands play the harp strings
of hotel shower streams
      I implore you:
           if you know me at all
           then do not speak.
Silence is the best storyteller.

Your eyelids spill over your eyes
like reluctantly crashing waves
      and I realize my mistake—   I cannot
           break anyone into their digestible parts;

I engulf and am engulfed by an endless sea
of non-linguistic sounds we know
but cannot speak.

We have always been concentric
circles   wholes
                drawn to the distant ocean
                sound of slow-breaking glass
                        the tires on ice and snow.

YOU WALKED TO THE GRILL IN MOCCASINS, BUT I HAD BARE FEET

Our food altar blooms between us
with pieces of what we eat
or may have discarded: a pinch of salt,
a soup spoon full of olive oil, a halved
bean. Ingredients on display
in the bowl with a museum's white walls.

You say I inspired this
after the ancestors ask me to simplify.
In sinking-sun candlelight, two stunted basil leaves,
red bell pepper seeds, a homegrown zucchini stem.
You don't have a table, so we eat cross-legged

on the floor and sit on opposite sides
of a knitted blanket from Goodwill. I move my glass
idly from one flower center
to the next in time with when you change
position. One Portobello mushroom chunk, asparagus,
a farm-picked Rainer cherry. We should have poured in
a drop of Tarima, my favorite Spanish wine I found

again after a year of searching; I couldn't remember
the name, only the firework flower on the bottle.
What will you do with the altar? *Compost,*
or maybe burn it. Quarterly.
You ask if I'm still hungry, but this suspended image
fills me completely.

WHEN BEING WOMAN IS METAPHOR

My scars aren't visible,
but I am paranoid all the same
before you arrive. I can't see you
through the window's reflection
from the hexagonal table
under coupon-clipped string lights.

You sit on the bench I chose
with blue spider-crab pillows
and an unaccommodating angle.
With one leg crossed at the ankle,
you look more comfortable in your skin
than anyone.
We drink Silver Needles on ice
for inner acupuncture
and talk of spheres until the green ivy
is greener in the evening sun.

I bike home
in a short, loose dress and leggings
while sidewalk cracks rumble with your tone:
wild, wild, wild.
I should have a helmet,
but I am childless and alive and maybe
the small of my back shows
as the wind picks up.

EPILOGUE

The poet will love everything about you: small tufts of stubborn grass outside your door, piles of mail hidden behind the fruit bowl, the fickle washing machine—which the poet insists on writing poems about. While the poet notices your details, there is blank space on the page the poet reserves for the rest of you. The poet does not pretend to understand.

If you ask the poet to write something about you, the result will be unflattering. If you don't ask, you will find yourself in everything the poet writes.

K. M. LIGHTHOUSE graduated from the University of Utah and worked as the senior poetry director of *enormous rooms* for two years but has since made the Pacific Northwest a home. The poet's other works appear in *From Sac*, *Blue Lake Review*, *Mapping Salt Lake City*, *Sonic Boom* and *Thought Catalog*. K. M. Lighthouse is an assistant organizer with Portland's Eastside Poetry Workshop and a member of High Priestesses of Poetry.

CPSIA information can be obtained
at www.ICGtesting.com
Printed in the USA
LVHW05s1101260718
584950LV00011B/205/P